An Unkindness of Ravens

An Unkindness of Ravens

✦✦

Poems by

~~Meg Kearney~~

[signature]

Foreword by Donald Hall

Brattleboro, VT
12/3/24

The A. Poulin, Jr. New Poets of America Series, No. 23

BOA Editions, Ltd. ✦✦ Rochester, New York ✦✦ 2001

The A. Poulin, Jr. New Poets of America Series, No. 23

Publications by BOA Editions, Ltd., a not-for-profit corporation under section 501 (c) (3) of the United States Internal Revenue Code are made possible with the assistance of grants from the Literature Program of the New York State Council on the Arts, the Literature Program of the National Endowment for the Arts, the Sonia Raiziss Giop Charitable Foundation, The Halcyon Hill Foundation, The Chase Manhattan Foundation, as well as from the Mary S. Mulligan Charitable Trust, the County of Monroe, NY, and The CIRE Foundation.

See Page 82 for Special Individual Acknowledgments

Cover Design: Lisa Mauro / Mauro Design
Art: "Antigone" from Antigone by Sophocles (oil on canvas) by Marie Spartali Stillman (1844–1927) courtesy of Simon Carter Gallery, Woodbridge, Suffolk, UK/Bridgeman Art Library
Interior Design: Bonnie Coen
Manufacturing: McNaughton & Gunn, Lithographers
BOA Logo: Mirko

LIBRARY OF CONGRESS CATALOGING-IN-PUBLICATION DATA

Kearney, Meg.
    An unkindness of ravens: poems / by Meg Kearney; foreword by Donald Hall.
        p. cm. — (The A. Poulin, Jr. new poets of America series; vol. 23)
    ISBN 1-929918-09-7 (pbk.: alk. paper)
    I. Title. II. Series.

    PS3611.E2 U55 2001
    811'.6—dc21   2001020213

BOA Editions, Ltd.
Steven Huff, Publisher
Richard Garth, Chair, Board of Directors
A. Poulin, Jr., President & Founder (1976–1996)
260 East Avenue
Rochester, NY 14604

www.boaeditions.org

unkindness: a flock (of ravens)

— *The Oxford English Dictionary*

Unkindness of Ravens: From the legend that ravens pushed their young from the nest to be "nourished with dew from heaven," as *The Folk Lore of British Birds* put it in 1885, until the adult birds "saw what colour they would be."

— James Lipton, *An Exaltation of Larks*

If in a shimmering room the babies came,
Drawn close by dreams of fledgling wing,
It was because night nursed them in its fold.

Night nursed not him in whose dark mind
The clambering wings of birds of black revolved,
Making harsh torment of the solitude.

— Wallace Stevens, "Palace of the Babies"

For my parents

CONTENTS

An Unkindness of Ravens

Redemption Arcade

Adoptive Measures

Foreword

Meg Kearney's *An Unkindness of Ravens* is a book of reticence and revelation, secrecy and surprise. Few poems are narrative, but something like a story emerges from these lyrics alive with hurt and splendor. Although the poems radiate personal feeling, we have no sense of confessional poetry as deliberate self-revelation; Kearney's confessional is Catholic. Some poems, especially the Raven series, derive from the recesses of dream; others observe the world from outside. Whatever place her poems come from, their beauty lies in their language. Accuracy and emotion speak through her passion for the right word, for the epithet that contains a universe — the "velvet hotels." With inventive wit she surprises: "I sing 'Amazing Grace' while Raven reclines at my feet, / painting my toenails." But if we laugh, we must laugh guardedly, for her poems — in their naked reticence, in their promiscuous innocence — bring us often to a frightening place. In her poem she observes the

                                        bottle
          of Cabernet brooding like a teenager
          in the front seat.

on her way to:

          Longing is a form of terror. It is
          the same woman hovering over postcards

          in a small White Mountain town. First
          you are surprised she has anyone
          to write home to. Then you realize maybe

          she's been following you. But that's
          impossible. Because this is your
          mother. She abandoned you long ago.

Some poems derive from childhood and enter into varieties of the erotic:

          I thought by now my
          body would demand less, not
          scream *I want, I want.*

Other poems embody the ambiguities of sexuality, which vibrate at the center of the human. "The Prodigal Daughter":

13

And so in the city's velvet hotels she
found all the men who longed to hold but could not keep her.
She asked for nothing, but her mind whispered *love me, love
me*. In bars dark as Burgundy one of them would reach across
the table for her hand, kiss each fingertip like a swollen
nipple, lick the inside of her wrist like a vulnerable thigh;
then she would take his finger into her mouth until he shouted
for the waiter to bring the check.

The next day the Daughter knows that she is "too bad for even Jesus / to love."

It's hard to know which poems to recommend most to the reader; her "14th Street" is an artful and moving sestina, exactly the form to represent the stymied protagonist. Here's the ending of "Creed":

and if you hold
your hand right here — touch me right
here, as if this is all that matters,
this is all you ever wanted, I believe
something might move inside me,
and it would be more than I could stand.

The movement of the last line, a countermovement that validates so many of these poems, embodies the necessary doubleness of the emotional life. And I would be remiss if I did not call attention to Kearney's ear, especially strong in its dance, its rythmic progress down the page to a resolution both intellectual and aesthetic.

Read "*La Belle Dame sans Merci*," "Loneliness," "Bonsai." Better, read straight through this remarkable first book.

— Donald Hall

An Unkindness of Ravens

Longing

Terror is a mirror in which your eyes belong
to a woman wearing sunglasses. There she is
now, pulling out of the parking lot across

the street in a new convertible, bottle
of Cabernet brooding like a teenager
in the front seat. Longing is that bottle

of wine you may never open. But there is
the woman again, lighting a cigarette
on the corner of Sixth and Twelfth.

St. Vincent wraps a shadow around her
shoulders as she flicks the cigarette
onto the ground and ducks into the dark

of Fat Tuesday's. You have spent years
following this woman across the city,
gathering her cigarette butts

and stuffing them into your mouth.
Longing is a form of terror. It is
the same woman hovering over postcards

in a small White Mountain town. First
you are surprised she has anyone
to write home to. Then you realize maybe

she's been following you. But that's
impossible. Because this is your
mother. She abandoned you long ago.

Gin

She came to sex as she'd come to gin. Five
years in the convent, what did she know
about gin? Sister Emmanuel said the Devil
himself was suckled on it, and after her
third drink in the Red Kilt she knew he was
inside her like a crazed Wizard of Oz,
pushing and pumping her levers and gears.
Each time she brought the glass to her lips,
Sister's voice whispered, You couldn't
lift one finger, not one pinky of one hand
if not for the love of God. But she was
twenty-five and didn't know anything about
love. She knew she wasn't holy, or chaste, or
even sorry. And she knew she was alone when
the man called her beautiful, when the gin
said, *Baby, relax, enjoy it while you can.*

Anything Else

When she gave up the baby the baby did not
cry, but she wished it would. She gave up her baby
by signing her name six times and they called it
surrendering. When it was born the baby had cried

immediately. That was the last time she had
heard it. The doctor in the coat white like
a chef's said, 6 pounds, 14 ounces, Apgar
10, a murmur, a hole in the heart that will heal

itself. The nurse said, Yes of course it hurts
to walk I'm sorry we cannot allow you to feed it,
and the woman, lying on the bed, did not
protest. The nurse was dressed in white so white

the woman had to close her eyes as the baby was taken
from her. *Too quiet — quiet baby aren't you hungry*
she thought though she could not keep anything
down. They tried to make her eat but all the food was

yellow, like the blanket they wrapped her baby in,
yellow blanket yellow booties as if the baby were
not born yet; as if the baby had nothing
to cry about, surrounded by sunny baby clothes,

sunny nurse faces. She had looked in the baby's eyes
and decided they would deepen to brown but remain
familiar. Now the woman stared at the empty
mound that was her belly, her arms' white fading

into white sheets, knowing down the hall a stranger
held the bottle and the baby sucked the rubber nipple,
took the nipple because it had no other choice,
because anything else would be a lie.

A Therapist Invites Me to Visit My Inner Child

I dread going back to see that girl
after her first day of kindergarten.
She is sitting on the front porch
of the green house on the hill
in her braids, freckles, and new plaid
dress. What should I not say?
The living-room drapes are drawn;
front door is closed against the afternoon
sun. The girl's socks are muddy. Her
pockets sag with diamonds she discovered
in the creek bed on the way home.
When Mother wakes from her nap,
the girl plans to give them to her.
She will stand by the couch
and pour into her mother's hands
diamonds that sparkle like ice in a glass.
Then her mother might be happy.
The girl is singing "Three Little Angels,"
waiting for those curtains to open.
I want to explain that once they dry,
the diamonds will be dull and gray.
I want her to stop singing that song.
I want to say her pockets are full of stones.

On Second Thought

— for my father

i

I was wrong about happiness. I thought
if I just knew where to look it would be
easily retrievable, like a hairbrush

I lost between the cushions of the couch
or the name of someone I used to know.
When did I stop knowing it? I thought

it would follow me when I left the house
in LaGrange, that like my childhood
memories happiness was safely contained

in the photograph of me and the neighborhood
kids wearing cone-shaped birthday hats with
elastic strings under our chins. But now

I look at those pictures and I think
about who took them. I think, I hated
how that string cut into my jaw, left

a temporary scar. I notice for the first
time the girl not eating cake, not
smiling in her black-and-gray though it must

have been yellow or red hat. I can't recall
her name, but wonder what she knew.
How, how did she know?

ii

I thought by now my
body would demand less, not
scream *I want, I want.*

21

iii

I was wrong to think language could save me,
or save you, for that matter. I see how
words are their own truth, while mine dies with me.

Once I believed childhood would be
a cross of gold around my neck, my own hallowed
relic. I wouldn't need language to save me.

I thought the body, I thought memory
would be dependable, that somehow, like words, they'd
form their own truth. But my truth dies with me

because I've written poems that might have made you
happy, but you'll never see. I realize now
I was wrong to think language could save me.
These words form their own truth. Mine dies with me.

iv

I was wrong about memory and the body.
I discover my hairbrush squeezed for months
in a crevice of the couch and find several
long, brown strands and one short, black,
graying — then I'm twenty-five again,
kneeling on the hospital bed gently brushing
his hair, saying, *Am I brushing too hard,*

Dad? Then let me use my brush. Saying,
You know I'm the only one with just the right
touch. Now, I pull his hair from my brush
and place it in my mouth. His cells break
down, become my own even before
I swallow. Tomorrow people will say,
You look so much like your father.

Loneliness

The girl hunting with her father approaches
the strange man who has stopped at the end
of his day to rest and look at the lake.
Do you like geese? she asks. The man smiles.
The girl draws a webbed foot from her pocket
and places it in his hand. It's late fall
and still the geese keep coming, two fingers
spread against a caution-yellow sky. Before
he can thank her, the girl has run off, down
to the edge of the water. The man studies her
father, about to bring down his third goose
today — then ponders the foot: soft, pink,
and covered with dirt like the little girl's hand.
He slides it into his coat pocket, and holds it there.

Family Vacation

I'm sitting on Daytona Beach with my bucket and shovel
and Gumby posture when my father asks me to smile, snaps
the picture. My hair is disobedient. From this angle, you
can see I've been eating too much banana bread and pecan
pie, and that the sand houses I've spent all morning building
and decorating are still unoccupied. Those families never
did show up, and now the walls are beginning to topple.

Soon it will be cocktail hour, time to pack the towels
and umbrella and walk back with my parents to the hotel.
I'll hang my damp suit on the balcony, then watch the kids
below splashing in the pool. I'll think about my little
houses, how the mommies and daddies finally arrived
with their babies, how they kissed each other and settled
in their beds just in time for the first, annihilating wave.

Antidote

When I reach the point of suffocation
I retreat to the room with three purple

walls, one lime green — to the monkey
filled with wheat pennies, horses with

broken legs, where the model ship and
miniature crew wait for me to take them

down from the shelf, and I wait for my
receiving blanket to catch fire, for

someone to emerge from the miniature
tepee stretched and stitched with

German leather. When the thunder stops
my dog will creep out from under the bed;

he cannot tell purple from green; he thinks
he'll live forever, though he doesn't

hear that woman outside my window,
always motioning for me to jump. I want

to unravel the knot of my navel and send
down the skin like a rope — but no,

forget her, let her rot out there; let her
disappear the usual way. Let me turn out

the light and dream I've grown gills,
bruised and purple on each side of my

neck, which sing impolitely at awkward
moments; dream the dog has cornered

Jesus in the yard — He's wearing a pea-green
sweater — and I'm small enough to walk

through an inch-high door into a world where
you love me, and you, and you and you.

The Prodigal Daughter

In her room overlooking the garden, she touched each thing
she could not pack: nine painted horses on a wooden shelf,
black-haired Dolly, eyes glued open by accident,
a glow-in-the-dark Jesus that hung on the wall beside her bed.

Down on her knees in the garden, she planted her finest treasure:
a glass seed, and a feather like a flag to mark its place. This
was the price of leaving. There is always a price, her mother
liked to say, God never promised you an easy life. Remember —

your body is His temple. But Jesus! She'd been taken by storm —
the money changers, tax collectors, cowboys, had all set up
their fly-by-night shops inside her and they were all such
terrible flirts. Besides, she knew no matter how far she wandered

from the garden or how late into morning she danced, no matter
how many goblets were smashed into the fire, how short her skirt
or a strange man's attention, more strangers would be waiting
to whisper their dying love, pour more wine, vow their terminal

affection for her body. And so in the city's velvet hotels she
found all the men who longed to hold but could not keep her.
She asked for nothing, but her mind whispered *love me, love
me*. In bars dark as Burgundy one of them would reach across

the table for her hand, kiss each fingertip like a swollen
nipple, lick the inside of her wrist like a vulnerable thigh;
then she would take his finger into her mouth until he shouted
for the waiter to bring the check. If the bar was in the hotel

it was all very simple: his hand rising inside her dress with
the elevator, key in the door, dress falling like a casualty
to the floor. If he was short, she took off her shoes. If he
was bald, she rubbed her breasts across his head, then kissed

it. If he begged, she often stayed until morning, washing
quietly in the bathroom while he phoned his sleepy wife,
cooed to his redheaded daughter. If this took a long time
she plundered his toiletries, found his shaving cream,

27

hummed while she lathered her cheeks and chin and upper lip,
then dragged a bent finger down her new face, each time rinsing
the foam from her hand under the hot tap, scraping, rinsing,
scraping until she heard the plastic drop of the receiver

in the next room, or until she could no longer bear it.
If later he slipped out of bed to the shower, scrubbing her scent
from his mustache and belly so that by daybreak
he could fly home to his clean house and a preoccupied wife

in Cincinnati or Salt Lake City, she'd hunt her scattered clothes
in the dark and go before he could see the price of freedom
dry and crusted on her face. She could wash him off, too,
in her own tub and wake up alone in her own reeking bed.

Those days she would sleep into the afternoon, then in a cotton
dress and sandals wander downtown, wondering if she should
eat something, or get her ear pierced again, or what
her father was thinking just then and what might be sprouting

in the garden, and if she was too bad for even Jesus
to love. In the church on Second Avenue she would light
a candle for her parents, and another because she hated
to see a candle not lit. On her way home she would

remember how, when she was young, she'd felt so light
after confession she could have floated away with
the altar boy's incense. Now innocence was a wide-eyed
doll sitting on her bed back home; now penance was

a dwindling option; there were too many things
she didn't regret. But she did finally seem to run out
of something she couldn't quite name. It had something
to do with desire; two years in the city and desire

had become a baby bird, beak open, waiting to be fed.
She knew there'd be a day when no one would come
to the nest. She didn't want to wait until she was alone,
too old to fly away. She could die with desire, or go home.

28

Home Movies

My father has been dead eight years before my mother and I can watch them again. There he is, waving to us from a black-and-white Christmas, pulling my sister on her new Flexible Flyer. She stands, takes his hand, and they free-fall backward, burning angels on a church-white lawn. The frame begins to jiggle with what must be my mother's laughter, and the scene shifts:

family in the living room, where movie lights blind us like love, and Martini Angel, spindled on the top of the tree, winks and careens. My brother has joined the scattered legion of toys on the floor — he sits on his hands, rocking, a G.I. Joe helmet guarding his crew-cut head against Mr. Machine and Gaylord the Walking Dog. The dog jerks to a stop, snaps twice at the air before my father's hands lift him, flip his off switch. I stand by the couch, fidgeting in my velvet dress, while Grandfather brushes my hair, mouths *Fröhliche Weihnachten* to my mother. And now, she does not look away from the screen when she says, He never touched me like that.

Silence

Nothing has changed after thirty-
nine years. The grown children
have come home for dinner. Each
sits in the usual seat, disliking
mushrooms, hogging the garlic
bread. They say grace, pass
the pepper. Salt has never been
allowed on this table, though
the youngest daughter will
fetch it from the kitchen cabinet
for a guest. Mother has barely
touched her food as she passes
the chicken and string beans
for a second time, urging, Eat.
Eat. Someone says Why don't you
eat. Someone says This is
delicious, and the rest nod.
Then the unsteady hand spills
the wine, a Rorschach test
spreading its red blotch across
the tablecloth. Each of them
sees the same thing. The phone
rings. They go on eating. Someone
says get a sponge. The phone
goes silent. Someone says
it might come out in the wash.

New York

I love the sharp smell of manure and sound of desolate
roads. But here I can study a subway map and be
everywhere at once; here a prime parking spot, a good
cheap restaurant, a quiet, rent-stabilized apartment make me
enticingly rich. Things like that don't count in LaGrange;

they count on a street where a man sleeps in a cardboard
box marked "stereo and misc"; they count in a hip
nightclub downtown where a woman dancing as slow
as a ballad on a backlit stage sings of her lost lover,
sings of how, when she finds him, life will be a slice

of heaven, and I believe her. Her voice is smoky
and abandoned like the roads back home; this is what
I'm thinking when the guy on the bar stool next to me says
something I don't quite hear. I glance at his tie and its repeating
diamonds; I'm wondering what happened to the woman's

lover and he repeats, Is it morning? His eyes look like two
martinis with olives. I reply, If she is, it becomes her.
He turns back to his drink so I don't explain that death,
the end of a body or end of love, is genuine — its pain, proof
you exist. Every time the lover gets on a train it's like

a little death. Her life is suddenly recognizable; her every
move — handing the ticket to the conductor, looking at her
watch, breathing in and out — is real, tangible. This, at
last, is her chance to feel. And so the train pulls away
and the man on the platform recedes, and she writes a poem about it.

The Trouble with Creation

Garden, pond,
man, woman,
worm
in the tequila,
salt licked
from the back
of his hand,
lemon squeezed
between bountiful
thighs, sunshine
on the tongue,
moonlight
on the water —
Come on in,
the water's
fine —
smoke in the belly,
apple in her eyes,
oh, forbidden
script, turn out
the lights,
pour us
another drink,
have some pie.

Bash Bish Falls

We'd planned to spend the night in the back of his van, but
as we climbed in I was saying how we really weren't so far
from home, and I was okay to drive. He said, Don't worry,
Baby, before he unzipped his jeans and pushed me down.

I heard Cathy, working her Junction Grill shift seven months
pregnant, warning, Don't swallow, which had struck me
as hilarious the week before but seemed so sad and weird
to think of then, on a mattress that screamed reefer and sex.

Was I supposed to like this? My best friend would've said,
That's how you become an adult. You fake it for a few years
till you figure out how to do it. But then I was on my back;
he was yanking my bathing suit away from my crotch, not

bothering to take it off. *Is this how? This?* I asked and asked
while he told me how good it felt, and how I deserved it.

Tea

Tomorrow the drinkers will dream in black and white
of their mothers and long-dead dogs, but right now
they've got a fridge full of beer, Jagger on the radio —
right now they've got themselves some coke, so

the party just went major league. Holding a Heineken
between his knees, J calls his girlfriend to say his car
won't start, this could take all night. It's August.
The body of the boy inside him flashes on the surface

and sinks. The screen door's littered with moths;
the refrigerator hums without taking a breath; an egg,
little smashed skull, rots at the bottom of the trash
can. A square white envelope shouts like a telegram

from the kitchen table. H keeps eyeing it, hoping his
wife stays out late so he won't have to share. *Fuck
the wife!* bellows P. He smells like the river, strokes
his beard, suggests *Let's smoke it.* J wipes his mouth

on his yellow Hawaiian shirt, then glances at H, who
nods. P lights the stove, rummages through a cabinet
for the pan, and fills it with water, while H disappears
to fetch the bong and mirror, the razor blade. Outside

a neighbor's dog barks twice, again — then yelps,
almost shrieks, falls silent. *This place reeks*, J grumbles
as he grabs another Heineken, but P ignores him.
He's thinking about the coke, already feeling his taste

buds heap their bodies on the back of his tongue.
Finally found a blade says H, stumbling in with
the bong. He cracked his first Bud at noon, same
time his wife got off the breakfast shift at the Acropolis.

She's down at Junior's betting on turtle races, chasing
tequila with Miller on tap. She yanks a thread from her
polyester skirt, checks her lipstick in a Captain Morgan
mirror, and cozies up to a suit-and-tie with twenties

stacked on the bar. Sometimes J's girlfriend stops here
after work, too, but tonight she's lying on the couch
in her panties and bra, sipping Jack Daniels, swearing
to her friend on the phone *This is the last time he's*

pulling this crap on me. She's already culled every
ashtray for enough roaches to roll one last joint. She'll
light it in the dark, then lie back against the cushions
and see how many times she can make herself come.

And J? He's still at his buddy's place thinking, One hit
and maybe I'll go home, but he studies P's hands
scraping the mirror, blade a snowplow banking its little
piles, and knows he's not going anywhere. *Did you clean*

the screen? asks P, his baseball cap slashed with fish
blood. P is sweating, as focused as a surgeon, when he
takes the first hit. His mind flips like cards in the spokes
of a wheel, his dead mother's face slaps in circles. And

he hadn't thought of his wife for a good hour, how she's
probably wrapped his dinner in tinfoil, or dumped it
in the garbage. That's her latest little revenge.
Sometimes she runs off for a day or two, but she comes

back. Yesterday she patched that rip in his jeans. By
this time she's brushed her hair, gone to bed with a mug
of tea and a book. Now and then she sets it down on her
lap, thinking she hears the car pulling into the driveway.

Learning to Speak

It wasn't I who scribbled M.S.K.
on the wall of the motel room
in blood-red lipstick, but a girl
who slipped out from our tangled
sheets after you fell asleep. She
rummaged through my purse
in the bathroom light, then
waited, clenching Passion Fire
in her fist, until I dressed,
kissed your forehead, and left.

The girl was afraid you would
forget me, that you would wake
to the empty room, a memory
of Pomerol still on your tongue,
and think only of the Blue Note,
the way Abbey Lincoln's neck
curved and throbbed in the jazz-
thick dark. The girl has spent
her life afraid to say something;
she is so well trained in the art

of reticence, the drama of disregard —
at this very moment she is practicing
what she will say when you decide
to call. She has locked herself
in the bathroom and written
her initials backward across
her forehead in red lipstick.
She stares into the mirror
rehearsing lines to tell you
It was me. It was me. It was me.

Swan Song

She knew by the way he shut the door when he got home.
She knew by the way he let the screen door slap
the heel of his work boot, rush of rain
on the porch while he fought the key out of the lock.

When he was high he would open the door real
slow, as if afraid of what he might find
inside his own house. As if he wouldn't wake her.
As if she could be sleeping at four in the morning
when he wasn't home yet. As if she wasn't awake
wondering whether he'd come home that day at all
or the next day and wishing he were dead.

When he was drunk he was clumsy and didn't care
about the racket he made, like this morning.
She could hear him pulling off his boots in the kitchen.
She knew his boots were full of mud. It had been raining
for days. When he came into the bedroom he dropped his
shirt on the floor. She felt him watching through the dark.

I'm soaked through, he said, unzipping his jeans.
He held on to the dresser with one hand, then the other
as he peeled them off, losing his balance,
recovering as he slapped the wet jeans on the chair
and rested both hands on the foot of the bed. She could
smell him now. Beer and cigarettes. He yanked down
the sheet that covered her and climbed onto the bed,

crawled his way up and over her. She looked at him,
then looked away as he leaned down to kiss her,
breath spilling onto her cheek. His cock was hard
and he was going to fuck her. She'd known this
by the way he'd come in the door. She could smell rain,
rain pouring in her head, in her lungs, in her mouth,
between her legs. Making a mess of everything.

Mrs. Plum, Outside the Library, with the Candlestick

My life thus far was found outlined in chalk
on Seventh Avenue. I lay down between the blue

lines, hugged my knees to my chest to test if it was
really me, then stood back smoking a Chesterfield

while the crowd gathered. They weren't interested
in who I was, but in the rumor of a woman gone wrong,

good girl seduced by Johnnie Walker Black — then
wronged again by a pimp without a profit, or a prophet

without a God. One thing we all knew: there's no
story without a body. I wanted to step into that

crowd, hold out my palms like Christ; I wanted
to dance flamenco with a stem of chalk in my

mouth. But it was beginning to rain, so I ducked
into the Italian place on Bleeker, ordered a bottle

of Chianti. I toasted the background music: *Once
Upon a Time in America.* I toasted the empty

woman on the sidewalk, and the rain that was,
at that very moment, sweeping her out to sea.

Fortune-Teller

The Gypsy hovers over her crystal so closely
her whorled face swims in votive light. "Here

is that little girl again, eating a bologna sandwich,"
she says. "It's summer, she's been swimming —

her braids drip like candles. Her tongue is orange."
Tang, I think. *The drink of astronauts.* "With one

hand, the girl holds a towel around herself, already
distrusting her body." "Who are you?" I ask. Yet

she continues: "The part in her hair is perfect."
"I could tell you a story about that," I offer, but

the Gypsy will not lift her face. "And here is a man,
swimming laps in a pool. The girl watches him

as she eats. His strokes are like a light beginning to
flicker. The girl is waiting for something to happen.

She wonders if she'll be strong enough to save him."
"Who are you?" I demand. "The girl wants so much

to look like him," she whispers. "Her eyes are the right
color, but already she is too tall. And now her scalp is

beginning to burn." I leap to my feet and the Gypsy,
startled, looks up at last. "Oh," I moan. "It's you."

39

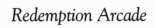

Redemption Arcade

Curse

The difference between a raven and a crow
is the intent of their blackness. The crow
is a raven's shadow. The crow is a memory
of a raven. Only a raven can transcend
the raven to become a prophecy.

We dream of crows but the raven lands in our bed,
wakes us wide-eyed and sweating rivers, rivers
of our body's water running hot between
our breasts, hot across our forehead and into
our own black hair.

It's a river I'm drowning in now, a river
fed by my own murder of crows, and I
alone can save me. Two thousand years ago
perhaps we rescued each other, and a thousand
years ago a raven slid between us.

Now here we are, clinging to opposite shores,
each reaching a hand out toward the river's
tongue, thinking somehow our tongues
might save us this time, break
the spell if we could just name it.

I wish I could talk beyond surviving, beyond
breathing, but I have a raven in my mouth,
I have a river in my lungs and no name
is coming to me, only blackness, the lateness
of the hour, the sound of wings beating.

Spending the Evening with Raven

I sing "Amazing Grace" while Raven reclines at my feet,
painting my toenails. He colors each toe green, then

begins over with red, blue, until each nail is black
as a corset. Don't call me Grace, he grumbles,

blowing the polish until it freezes, threatens
to chip. His breath spills up my leg, wicking hair to

hair until I stop it with my hand at my upper thigh.
When will you forgive me? I demand. Color me

penitent, daughter of a nun. Paint my name backward
across my forehead, then let me look into your eyes.

Raven buffs each nail like a tiny patent leather
shoe, works so furiously he renders himself

invisible. *Keep singing*, I hear, as the bottle
of Patient Purple shivers, then disappears.

What She Told Me

Sometimes the raven talks in its sleep.
Once, it said
Not enough.
Once, it said
Oh, Mother.
Once it caught me hovering
over its trembling beak, my ear so close
I feared I might fall.
It shook my hair from its eyes; we
were perched in a tree and below
the city shivered.
I could smell the dead
the raven had eaten for breakfast. Its back
was purple, red, then white; its back
was a room, a chapel dimly lit
where a woman was crying. I thought
I knew her; her eyes were hazel. I almost
called her name, but she hurried away,
slipping a photograph of me
into her pocket.

Dreaming of Raven

Doors part like eyelids: I am standing
on the side of Titusville Road, the corner
that's killed seventeen dogs, nine cats,
and Sue Studley's father. Behind me lies
the ditch where they toss unclaimed
animals. Something is moving down there
like a priest on yesterday's battlefield.
Already the smell is unbearable.

It's not a priest and it's not alone;
huddled together in a ditch seven ravens
can be mistaken for a cassock. They are
performing their last rite: looting
and the feast that follows. And there
is a woman moving among them; I know her
eyes are hazel, though I cannot see them.
This is not a burial ground, but
a cause for celebration. I hear
eyes popping like balloons.

Down the road past Keller's house
I wander into a field. This is not
supposed to be here, this pale grass, this
bench, what my parents wanted instead
of a headstone so we could sit at their grave
and eat lunch. I cannot rest here
with these feathers tangled among weeds
like black lupine. *No one can rest
here*, I cry, sitting on the bench,
wearing my mother's wedding dress.

Redemption Arcade

Behind me, the man with two mouths is trading
autographed Bibles for shots of sacramental

wine. He sucks from a nippled bottle with one
mouth, while the other speaks in tongues.

Raven is hearing confessions behind a fun
mirror in the House of Tricks; the woman

in line ahead of me has twisted her hair
into knots of Hail Marys. I say them

with her until it is her turn to go. Off
in the video games, electronic church bells

flash and chime as Sister Mary Margaret breaks
the coffers on *The Last Temptation of Christ*.

This place is a virtual blessing! cries the woman
exiting the confessional, her face sliding

like a medallion down her neck and between
her breasts, where it disappears, mouthing

a prayer. Raven flies out of the booth
squawking with rage, dives after the relic

as the woman swoons, collapses in my arms —
I steal a glimpse down her blouse, where

I see myself at age ten on a miniature midway,
about to take candy from a stranger.

Martini Angel

Raven is perched on my Christmas tree
where Angel used to sit, sipping
martinis on the sly. We called her
"the Martini Angel," though she kept
her gin hidden with the rest of the liquor

in the house. She always tilted to one
side like a caroler on a binge, her
flustered white hair a constant surprise.
Lit from within, her familiar face
blinked unpredictably. Look! the adults

would laugh, swirling ice in their
glasses — Angel's been in it again!
But Angel's had one Christmas too many.
I imagine she's out dancing at some
nightclub with the shepherd boy, who

leaned against the manger door
on account of his missing leg. Or she's
flown off with Melchior, the gold-bearing
king, who's keeping her in gin and cocktail
onions, skewered on those tiny plastic

swords. I console myself: at least Raven
is a sober substitute. But I'm no angel,
he reminds me, swaying back and forth
on the treetop singing "Rock-a-Bye
Baby." Raven nudges my hand-painted

birds, watches with glee as they drop
to the floor, crack like his voice — Oh,
the legacy of a thousand mothers! he
cries, as I sit on the floor turning
blue with all the other babies.

Encounter

What is the sound of a raven burning?
The position of the sun
is your only clue. At dusk
the air darkens with each breath.
You cock your head to one side;
essence of raven fills your body.

You move closer, you hear fire
taking wing. What
does it sound like?
A gust of sighs the color of a bruise.
Closer still, this unkindness
singes your eyelashes, the back

of your throat. Black eyes
pierce your hands. You hear
your own flesh burning as you drop
and roll with the bird,
desperate to douse the flames —
but your attempt is foolish;

you are suddenly more alone
than you ever expected. There is
nothing under your body but
an absence of light. The sun is
rising now over your shoulder
and you stare at your filthy

hands. Your stigmata have
disappeared, leaving only
two small scars
in the shape of a bird.
A shadow flies behind you
and hides itself in your shoes.

What the Dream Reveals to Him

Tonight he dreams again of the woman with ravens in her hair.
On the floor beside the bed, his dog whimpers in its sleep.

How many nights will the woman becken from her verdant ledge;
how many ravens will it take until he offers them his hands,

until his fingers run black with the darkness of her, until
his lips learn the song beating its black wings in her throat?

How many ravens will it take until he succumbs to his craving
for the sweet flesh of the tongue, the liver, the vulnerable

belly? The man moans, stretches one uncertain hand to the empty
room. His dog stirs, chasing its own elusive birds. The dog

will never come to love them. But the man opens his eyes, sensing
the woman is not far, knowing that to kiss her he must call

ravens to nest on his shoulders. Knowing that to love her
he must tear the raven in two and begin eating.

Adoptive Measures

Love Is a Form of Recklessness

My mother is AWOL from God.
That's what the nuns back
in Bristol are whispering,
though they're not allowed
to speak her name or listen
to the radio, which keeps on
playing the summer of '64's
number-one hit on the pop charts:
Dionne Warwick's "Walk on By."

My mother's left hand grips
the steering wheel; her right
rubs her chin as Dionne belts
that line, "Oh, foolish pride...."
Mother's Levi's are still too
tight. Her hair is snarled above
her neck; her heart's a key on
a kite string. She left the convent
two years before and still has

nothing, not even her baby.
The alto horn cuts in, Dionne's
backup, as my mother,
twenty-five and broke, drives
her parents' Chevy back
to Long Island. I'm left in
Manhattan, seven days old and
clueless but panicky, because
I'd sensed her panic as she left,

her kisses a pillow pressed to my
mouth. Now she wants to change
the station, change her mind,
because chances are she won't
recognize me if, years later,
I walk by her on the street. My
mother's love is the strength
to walk and keep on walking,
drive and keep driving until

her daughter has learned to live
without her, until the day
a chance meeting is impossible
because she is forty-four and soon
will be dead. But my mother does
not see that far ahead. She merges
onto the L.I.E., reaches down,
turns up the volume on the radio,
and begins to sing along.

La Belle Dame sans Merci

Her voice was songbird blue; her hair,
bedroom black, and men didn't know which
to love or which to fear. But when they
had to make a choice, it was what she
lacked they blamed her for, and so could
turn their backs guilt-free. If only
she could explain, it was all that singing,
it was all that wild honey, but more it was
those knights, one after another pulling her
onto the horse, asking her to sing — always
with that line, Has anyone ever told you...?
Then soon enough the two would come upon
that hillside where late in the day the dew
was stubborn, and here he'd beg for mercy.
Then sleep. Was it mercy they sought, or
pity? Later, she wasn't sure; she'd run out
of both for herself before she'd run out of
either for them. Even when there seemed to be
nothing left in her to give she managed
to find a drop or two of something — until
at last she'd given it all away, and when
the knight awoke, she was gone. Gone,
just like that! he told his friends
at The Mermaid. They nodded, full of pity,
and said they too had been victim of that
bitch, that tease. And the knight, feeling
so much better, ordered drinks all around.

The Prodigal Mother

She cannot enter the house.
No one has come out to greet her,
to say she is forgiven, to say
there will be roast lamb, dancing —

no one knows she's dropped her
suitcase on the porch, slipped back
to the garden where splinters of glass
quiver in the twilight, weeds and glass

everywhere, as if a crystal ball
had sprouted, then burst with what
it knew. And here is Molly, face-
down in the dirt, legs sprawled,

lace petticoat revealing a torn
thigh. Have you no modesty, Molly?
She embraces the doll, glances up
toward her broken window. It's

getting dark. No one is home to turn
on the lights. The woman sits down
in the dirt, thinking of Jesus. Molly,
slumped on her lap, stares into her

own empty chest. Too much sun has
faded her hair. So many hands have
touched her, she can't even close her
eyes and pretend she's somebody else.

Violet

What makes her stick her finger down her throat
has nothing to do with red wine or rancid meat
or the doughnuts and second bowl of chocolate mocha

chip, or how she was taught to finish what she
started, or the little black bird that perches
on her windowsill each morning. When the woman

wakes she looks for him, then beyond to the field
where the boy is galloping in circles, wanting
a horse so bad he has become the horse, whose

side he swats with his palm, Faster! Faster! But
the bird pecks at the glass, so the woman dresses,
brews coffee, drives to work. Every time she

brings the bagel, the sandwich, the spaghetti
to her mouth she thinks of the bird, how black he
is, how violet. She wishes he could come with her

to the office, sit on her shoulder. Everyone would
admire him. She would feed him bits of bologna,
crumbs of cookie; she would stroke his oily head,

his feathers like satin, like pitch, carnal and
starless. He would peck at her ear and pull her
hair so she would not fall into the empty space

that sucks her in, where she is wretched,
sterile, where it is impossible to
breathe — no, he would sink his claws into

her skin; he would wake her every morning without
fail, and she would be immaculate. He would
devour what is vile inside her, and say he loves it.

She Tries to Go to Confession

The priest has spent all day in the field
of strawberries, congregations of savage
hearts beating in June heat. God's servant,
he gathers them in his basket, weeping,
juice streaming down his chin.

Now he knows it is late — the acolyte has
lit the candles; the stained-glass Jesus
has grown somber; three or four confessors
are surely in line already, and she is last
among them, shifting from foot to delicate foot.

Father is in the mood for a party. He sings,
dances a little jig between the rows, berries
bouncing and bruising as plundered hearts will
do. The church line grows. A foot begins to tap.
Let them wait, he thinks. *Let's see who'll wait.*

What It's Like

I'll try to tell you only because of that song you wrote,
because of your lost son, because you noticed me searching
your face and stroking my chin, and you said, Do that again,
it's okay. That's part of what it's like. I search faces
on the street, at the supermarket, laundromat; I try
not to be rude; I stroke my chin — Do I have your nose?
Would you turn your head? Do you have this little point
on your right ear? Do you like milk in your coffee, but
only in the afternoon? Do you know Yeats by heart? Does
Whitman make you do a little dance? Do you like music?

Chopin calms me: the piano tastes like Cabernet, it smells
like buttered popcorn, then it smells like bread, it makes
the knots in my shoulders relax a little. Sometimes the music
feels so safe I lie down on the floor, belly up like a cat
who trusts her world completely. Jazz makes me tremble — all
that freedom, all those risks, those loose threads threatening
to pull and never stop unraveling — if I listen too long I
begin to fall. I weep so easily. It's hard enough clinging
to this floor, not tumbling into that hole in the ceiling
where there's not even a night sky to catch me.

Candlelight quiets the chatter in my head, all those monkeys
gabbling at once telling me *Be good! Be good! Don't
tell; don't don't.* In a candlelit room there's a possibility
of starting all over again; it's what it must feel like to be
born — all that watery light, and there, on the wall,
a woman who could be my mother. As long as I stay here
with the candles, she won't disappear. There's a possibility
you might see me here, I mean really *see* me — though please
don't ask me where I'm from. It's an unreachable place
where wind has worn everyone's face away; it's a child's
tea party where you just pretend to eat the cookies.

Are you beginning to feel what I feel? I practice and I
practice, but my prayers are not grateful enough; they're
mustard seeds though they should be forest fires, so
hot, so smoky all the monkeys stampede and there's

nothing left at the end when it all clears but a place
where the earth is rich and humming like a saxophone's
throat, where I can let that music fly because I'm up
to my knees in it, where there are people beside me
tapping their feet and no one's threatening to leave;
where I can turn to you and say, After this tune maybe you
will play that song again, and It's okay if my eyes don't
look like yours because I've never felt so much at home.

Sculpture of Gulls

They are riding the crest of a wave that never quite
breaks. One gull flies just above the other
and slightly behind, as if he could protect his
mate from the past or a possible fury
overhead, disguised now as a cloud, white as sea.
She worries more about what lies ahead, the beach
and its dependable shifting, the huge blue
swell beneath her, the depth of its insatiable
thirst. What they know about the wind holds them.
What they are learning about each other
makes them cry out, startled.

14th Street

In the apartment next door, a boy plays the piano —
Chopin, mostly, though sometimes notes he's made up.
Through the woman's window climbs the incessant noise of 14th Street:
merciless horns, squealing bus brakes, carnival-like music
from an ice cream truck, permanently parked, belting "She'll Be Comin' 'Round
the Mountain" over and over and over.

The phone rings; her lover coos, Can I come over?
She hesitates, weighs her desires: company, or listening to the piano,
spending the evening with her books. Can you come around
nine? she concedes. How about eight, he counters. I'll cook up
some pasta, open the red Bordeaux, put on a little music —
Eight-thirty, she sighs. Pick up some bread at Palermo's on 14th Street.

She settles on the couch with *Take Heart* by Molly Peacock. 14th Street
begins to fade like an old grief. She turns the book over;
the cover: "Hummingbird & Passion Flowers;" inside: the music
of poetry, intelligent passion of form, not so unlike the piano
sonata walking through her wall like a ghost. Up-
stairs a neighbor screams for quiet. The ice cream truck begins another round.

How many times can one listen to "She'll Be Comin' 'Round
the Mountain"? How *could* a woman ride six horses at once? 14th Street
is no place for country songs, or a girl from LaGrange. Up
where she's from they play a song once, and then it's over.
She closes the window, eases back on the couch. The piano
overwhelms the noises of the street; she can return to her poems, the true music.

In "Blue and Huge," Peacock describes the ocean: "It's like music,
a substance that can't be cut up." The woman smiles. Unlike a round
that divides a card game, the ocean doesn't end by chance. The piano
is silent. She doesn't notice, so absorbed even 14th Street
can't touch her. She uses sticky notes to mark poems she will read over.
Just then, the door buzzer. He croons, Can I come up?

She's regretting their date. I'm not sure I'm up
to this tonight, she says as he selects a CD, puts on some music.
He pulls her toward him. Are you saying it's over

between us? he teases, knowing how to bring her around.
She presses closer, confides: I guess I have to get away from 14th Street.
Relax, he whispers. It's just you and me, and Monk on the piano.

Later, alone in bed, she wonders if her mother's still up.
It's too late to call. She can't sleep, keeps replaying that street music,
imagining a girl riding six white horses, over and over and over.

Why God Asked Solomon the Question, and Not Me

Imagine God, shaking you from sleep and asking
What do you want? Just the thought makes me
salivate like a dog, makes me realize
what an animal I am. Unlike Solomon, I'm not
wise enough to want wisdom or goodness
of heart. Not that I'm greedy — I don't need
the king's ransom, Little Dipper of diamonds
curling around my ear; I know too much about
attachments and loss to want to live forever.
I don't want to be the Queen of Sheba or
Greta Garbo. I want what the dog has:
a hand warm with its own need caressing
my pale, horizontal back; a baritone voice
cooing, Good girl...beautiful girl. I want to lick
and be licked; desire unleashed, panting, sticky
and smelling of hair; understanding at a pitch
only a dog can hear.

Bonsai

You carry the tree home to me
like a baby from a house about
to burn. It was the potential
for fire that drew me to you,

though now, as you hand over
this gift I've longed for, I
worry if I can share my life
with something else so needy.

I study the instruction book: direct
light, lots of water, human breath,
and, every day, hands placed on
the moss at the base of the trunk.

Touch. Talk. I can do this. I am
determined this tree will live,
though when I discover aphids, tufts
of cotton caught in the leaves

like tiny laundry blown by a storm,
I panic, pick up the phone —
I am not afraid to say I need
help. The woman at the nursery

calms me: This happens, she says. Don't
worry so much. I try — yet spraying
insecticide, I think if junipers had eyes,
this one would be crying like a child

in the tub. I'm told I did the same
as a baby — screamed as my mother
scrubbed my face raw, baffled by
the indelible dirt on my cheeks

until my sister, to my rescue,
realized they were freckles.

My mother never had a child
with freckles until I came along,

as I never had a bonsai with brown
spot — another phone call and soon I'm
mixing vitamins, spraying for lush color,
praying for leaves that spring back

when squeezed between forefinger and thumb.
When I must go away, I call long-distance —
Is it drinking enough, getting lots of sun?
Don't leave it in the sink unattended;

it likes to be read to. I need you to say
everything is going to be all right,
say the tree is fine. Your voice across
the wire is a rain I've needed

for years; I tilt back my head,
softening into a girl only you have
recognized. The tree's body contains
what I can't yet explain.

When I am home, you pick me up, carry
me to the bedroom. Your skin smells
faintly of juniper. We burst in a heat
so green it singes my eyelashes.

Prologue to True Love:
Chopin's Waltz in A Minor, Op. 34, No. 2

The house is on fire,
yet the couple keeps
dancing. Her hand

on his shoulder, his palm
against the small of her
back can't keep the music

from ending. Her filigreed
gown is tarnished, his
tuxedo's come unstitched.

Soon they must pass
through the blazing door,
follow all those others

into the indifferent
street. Only Ashkenazy
will remain. He will

climb onto his piano
and lie down, ready
to admit the house

had always been
on fire, roof just
about to collapse.

Doppelgänger

Most people bring her out like a mailman brings out
the dog, but she's been shy around you. She's been
burning all my love letters behind my back while
Beethoven's Sonata No. 30 urges her on. Nothing
can shatter that finale's simple abandonment —

it's so seductive it lured even her into view:
see her now? Note her freckled skin, falling
shoulders. She wishes she weren't this tall,
wishes you wouldn't stare. She knows she's not
pretty; she's overweight — but she'll earn

straight A's, scrub the toilet, keep your ugliest
secret. Her longing is a stuffed black
dog who sleeps with her in a fetal curl. She
whispers in my ear, *Remember when we were eight,
in our room with just Molly and Monkey Sam?*

And I reply, *We don't have to go there anymore.*
Then I restart Beethoven; music is the only thing
that soothed her until you came along. Do you
remember the night I sat outside your door while
you played "Julia" on your guitar? It was twenty

degrees and snowing and I was trembling in an
unfamiliar heat. Your music wove a wreath of daisies
around my head as if it were April, while she stood
shivering behind me, yanking out one petal at a time,
murmuring, *He Loves You Not, He Loves You Not.* Then

you surprised us, opening the door — you, astonished
to see us, too — light splashing from your room into
winter like milk, like everything safe I had ever
known, everything she mistrusts, and she left me,
her pockets blooming, and I haven't seen her since.

Falling in Love at the Aquarium

— after a painting by Michael Filan

Van Gogh sang a cappella in the iridescent light
where fish bloomed in a field of tourmaline
green. Our tongues turned to sugar through that
deluge of saltwater ruby, undertow of tropical
glass, until nothing made sense beyond a silent
code of sea grass melting across a thick
buttered vista. You turned as if to ask, *What
is the sound of an oyster-shell sunrise?* So
I turned into a pearl, hid myself in your hands.

Ticket

I have a ticket in my pocket that will take me from Lynchburg
to New York in nine hours, from the Blue Ridge to Stuy Town,

from blue jays wrangling over sunflower seeds to my alarm
clock and startled pigeons. If I had a daughter I'd take her

with me. She'd sit by the window wearing the blue dress
with the stars and sickle moons, counting houses and cemeteries,

watching the knotted rope of fence posts slip by while I sat
beside her pretending to read, but unable to stop studying

her in disbelief. Her name would tell her that she's beautiful.
Belle. Or something strong, biblical. Sarah. She would tolerate

the blue jay and weep for the pigeon; she would have all the music
she wanted and always the seat by the window. If I had a daughter

she would know who her father is and he would be home writing letters
or playing the banjo, waiting for us, and I would be her mother.

We'd have a dog, a mutt, a stray we took in from the rain one night
in November, the only stray we ever had to take in, one night in our

cabin in the Catskills. It would be impossibly simple: two train tickets;
a man, a dog, waiting; and a girl with her nose pressed to the window.

Elegy for the Prodigal Mother

I used to think you were a spy, but
realize now you just lost your conviction

for the Passionate Sisters in Bristol.
That explains your burrito-and-cherry-

coke novenas, the way you cut your habit
into street clothes. It wasn't enough

to escape as far as Boston or Kings
Park or Tucson. You stood in the desert

like a saguaro; you banged at the gate;
you tripped them up on their own trick

question. Like you, I confuse longing with
mercy: how you sent your turquoise cross

skidding across my floor, caressed my face
in the dark when you thought I was sleeping.

Creed

I believe the chicken before the egg
though I believe in the egg. I believe
eating is a form of touch carried
to the bitter end; I believe chocolate
is good for you; I believe I'm a lefty
in a right-handed world, which does not
make me gauche, or abnormal, or sinister.
I believe "normal" is just a cycle on
the washing machine; I believe the touch
of hands has the power to heal, though
nothing will ever fill this immeasurable
hole in the center of my chest. I believe
in kissing; I believe in mail; I believe
in salt over the shoulder, a watched
pot never boils, and if I sit by my
mailbox waiting for the letter I want
it will never arrive — not because of
superstition, but because that's not
how life works. I believe in work:
phone calls, typing, multiplying,
black coffee, write write write, dig
dig dig, sweep sweep. I believe in
a slow, tortuous sweep of tongue
down the lover's belly; I believe I've
been swept off my feet more than once
and it's a good idea not to name names.
Digging for names is part of my work,
but that's a different poem. I believe
there's a difference between men and
women and I thank God for it. I believe
in God, and if you hold the door
and carry my books, I'll be sure to ask
for your name. What is your name? Do
you believe in ghosts? I believe
the morning my father died I heard him
whistling "Danny Boy" in the bathroom,
and a week later saw him standing in
the living room with a suitcase in his

hand. We never got to say good-bye, he
said, and I said I don't believe in
good-byes. I believe that's why I have
this hole in my chest; sometimes it's
rabid; sometimes it's incoherent. I
believe I'll survive. I believe that
"early to bed and early to rise" is
a boring way to live. I believe good
poets borrow, great poets steal, and
if only we'd stop trying to be happy
we could have a pretty good time. I
believe time doesn't heal all wounds;
I believe in getting flowers for no
reason; I believe "Give a Hoot, Don't
Pollute," "Reading is Fundamental,"
Yankee Stadium belongs in the Bronx,
and the best bagels in New York are
boiled and baked on the corner of First
and 21st. I believe in Santa
Claus, Jimmy Stewart, Zuzu's petals,
Arbor Day, and that ugly baby I keep
dreaming about — she lives inside me
opening and closing her wide mouth.
I believe she will never taste her
mother's milk; she will never be
beautiful; she will always wonder what
it's like to be born; and if you hold
your hand right here — touch me right
here, as if this is all that matters,
this is all you ever wanted, I believe
something might move inside me,
and it would be more than I could stand.

Notes and Dedications

"Antidote": The first line is borrowed from Gerald Stern's poem "When I Have Reached the Point of Suffocation," from *This Time: New and Selected Poems*, W. W. Norton, 1998.

"Loneliness" is for Donald Hall.

"What It's Like" is for Paul Reisler.

"Falling in Love at the Aquarium" is dedicated to Michael Fleming.

"Elegy for the Prodigal Mother": In Hebrew, "Elizabeth" is translated as "God's solemn oath."

"Creed" was inspired by Jack Wiler's poem "Belief System."

Acknowledgments

I am grateful to the editors of the following publications in which a number of these poems (some in earlier versions) first appeared:

Black Warrior Review: "What She Told Me"
The Brownstone Review: "Encounter"
Desperate Act: "Curse"
DoubleTake: "What It's Like"
The Florida Review: "Elegy for the Prodigal Mother"
Free Lunch: "The Prodigal Daughter"
The Gettysburg Review: "Prologue to True Love: Chopin's Waltz in A Minor, Op. 34, No. 2"
Mind the Gap: "Home Movies," "Redemption Arcade," "Spending the Evening with Raven"
Pivot: "Sculpture of Gulls," "Why God Asked Solomon the Question, and Not Me"
Ploughshares: "14th Street"
Poetry in Performance 25: "What the Dream Reveals to Him"
64: "Love Is a Form of Recklessness," "Ticket"
Sycamore Review: "Learning to Speak"
Tar River Poetry: "On Second Thought"
Third Coast: "Silence"
Washington Square: "She Tries to Go to Confession"

I am deeply indebted to Michael Fleming, Marion Quinn, Meg Dunn, Deborah Smith-Bernstein, George Drew, Donald Hall, William Matthews, Laure-Anne Bosselaar, Kurt Brown, Steve Huff, Thom Ward, Cornelius Eady, Neil Baldwin, Jennifer Kroll, Mel Rosenthal, Bobbe Perry-Mapp, Rick Pernod, Judith Baumel, and Wayne Koestenbaum for their inspiration, editorial assistance, generous spirits, and belief in me as a poet. I am also grateful to the Virginia Center for the Creative Arts, where I was able to complete this book's manuscript.

About the Author

Meg Kearney is the Associate Director of the National Book Foundation, headquartered in New York City. Before joining the Foundation in 1994, she organized educational programs and conducted power plant tours for a gas-and-electric utility in Upstate New York.

A former poetry editor of *Echoes*, a quarterly literary journal, Kearney is also past president of the New York State Hudson Valley Writers Association. She was the recipient of fellowships to the Virginia Center for the Creative Arts in 1998, 1999, and 2000. In 2001, she received an Artist's Fellowship from the New York Foundation for the Arts. She received a *New York Times* Fellowship and the Alice M. Sellers Academy of American Poets Prize in 1998, and the Geraldine Griffen Moore Award in Creative Writing in 1997, all from The City College of New York; and the Frances B. DeNagy Poetry Award in 1985, from Marist College in Poughkeepsie, New York. A student of the late William Matthews, she completed her Master of Arts Degree in Creative Writing at The City College, City University of New York, in 1999.

Kearney was born in Manhattan and grew up in LaGrange, seventy-five miles north of New York City. She now lives in Manhattan with her husband, writer Michael Fleming.

BOA Editions, Ltd.
The A. Poulin, Jr. New Poets of America Series, No. 23

Colophon

The publication of this book was made possible by the special support of
the following individuals:

Deborah Smith-Bernstein & Martin B. Bernstein
Diann Blakely
Laure-Anne Bosselaar & Kurt Brown
Nancy & Alan Cameros
Dr. William & Shirley Ann Crosby
Dane & Judy Gordon, Richard & Mimi Hwang
Peter & Robin Hursh, Robert & Willy Hursh
Boo Poulin, Deborah Ronnen, David Ryon
Peter Saunders & George Sommer
Jett & Shelley Whitehead
Pat & Michael Wilder

An Unkindness of Ravens was set in Goudy and Adobe woodtype
fonts by Bonnie Coen, LeRoy, New York
Cover design is by Lisa Mauro / Mauro Design, Rochester, New York
Art: *"Antigone" from Antigone by Sophocles* (oil on canvas)
by Marie Spartali Stillman, (1844–1927) Simon Carter Gallery,
Woodbridge, Suffolk UK/Bridgman Art Library
Manufacturing was by McNaughton & Gunn, Saline, Michigan

A special, limited edition of *An Unkindness of Ravens* was bound in
quarter cloth and French papers over boards, numbered 1–50,
and signed by Meg Kearney and Donald Hall.